TOO BUSY
NOT
TO PRAY

Journal

BILL HYBELS

with Carolyn Nystrom

InterVarsity Press
Downers Grove, Illinois

InterVarsity Press
P.O. Box 1400, Downers Grove, IL 60515, USA
World Wide Web: www.ivpress.com
E-mail: mail@ivpress.com

*InterVarsity Press®, U.S.A., is the book-publishing division of InterVarsity Christian
Fellowship/USA®, a student movement active on campus at hundreds of universities, colleges and
schools of nursing in the United States of America, and a member movement of the International
Fellowship of Evangelical Students. For information about local and regional activities, write Public
Relations Dept., InterVarsity Christian Fellowship/USA, 6400 Schroeder Rd., P.O. Box 7895, Madison,
WI 53707-7895.*

All Scripture quotations, unless otherwise indicated, are taken from the Holy Bible, New
International Version®. NIV®. *Copyright ©1973, 1978, 1984 by International Bible Society. Used
by permission of Zondervan Publishing House.*

Cover photograph: Comstock, Inc.
ISBN 0-8308-1973-8 (pbk.)

Printed in the United States of America ∞

19	18	17	16	15	14	13	12	11	10	9	8	7	6	5	4	3	2	1
13	12	11	10	09	08	07	06	05	04	03	02	01	00	99	98			

Getting the Most out of the *Too Busy Not to Pray Journal*

I call on you, O God, for you will answer me;
  give ear to me and hear my prayer.
Show the wonder of your great love,
  you who save by your right hand.
P S A L M   17:6-7

One of the best ways to grow in prayer is to write your prayers to God. It helps keep you focused while you are in prayer. And it's great to have a record of God's faithfulness and your spiritual growth!

This book is designed to help you get started in the discipline of prayer and journaling. It serves as a companion to *Too Busy Not to Pray.* Reading the chapters of that book along with these exercises will reinforce the principles you are practicing.

There are a number of different types of ideas in this book.

 Write. These sections provide encouragement to reflect on your past and current experiences in prayer by the process of journaling.

Reflect. Scripture and excerpts from *Too Busy Not to Pray* along with key questions will inspire and encourage you to reflect on what you are learning about prayer in your personal experience.

Study. Key passages to read, accompanied by questions, will help you dig deeper into the biblical meaning of prayer.

 Prayer Journal. Writing out your prayers to God will help you look at how to pray and what you pray. You'll be encouraged as you read your prayers to see how you are growing. You can also reread these prayers aloud as worship to God.

 Record. These sections structure the discipline of remembering specifically who you pray for and what you pray about. They will allow you to see God's continuing presence in your life.

Most likely, you will want to complete one exercise at a time. (The icons mark new exercises.) You may, however, prefer to spend a half day in study and prayer, going through one chapter along with the book. Use this guide freely in the way you learn best.

After you complete each chapter, you may want to talk about what you are doing with a friend or a small group. There are discussion questions at the back of *Too Busy Not to Pray* that draw out the key principles of each chapter. Additionally, *Prayer: Too Busy Not to Pray* provides six Bible studies to accompany some of the chapters. These studies are great for a group as well as for individuals.

Not everything in this journal is planned. Fill it in with prayers or thoughts from your daily life or favorite quotes and songs. This book is meant to inspire and encourage you, so use it as you wish.

1

God's Presence, God's Power

 **Write.** In the middle of the bleakest night I have ever known after my father's death, one overpoweringly intimate moment with God gave me courage, reassurance and hope. God simply said, "I'm able. I'm enough for you. Right now you doubt this, but trust me."

❄   ❄   ❄   ❄

Write about a time that you have experienced God's comfort through prayer.

**Reflect.** The most intimate communion with God comes only through prayer. Philippians 4:6-7 says:

Do not be anxious about anything, but in everything, by prayer and petition, with thanksgiving, present your requests to God. And the peace of God, which transcends all understanding, will guard your hearts and your minds in Christ Jesus.

❊   ❊   ❊   ❊

How does this Scripture speak to needs you have in your life?

Hear my prayer, O LORD;
  listen to my cry for mercy.
In the day of my trouble I will call to you,
  for you will answer me.

P S A L M 86:6-7

❊   ❊   ❊   ❊

How do you feel when you read that God will answer you?

 **Study.** People are drawn to prayer because they know that *God's power* flows primarily to people who pray. How would you describe the relationship between prayer and God's power?

❉   ❉   ❉   ❉

Read Matthew 5:44-45. What do these verses tell you about prayer and God's power?

_____

_____

Read Romans 8:26-27. How do we know what to pray?

_____

_____

What do you see as the role of the Holy Spirit in prayer?

_____

_____

_____

What are some ways we might experience God's power as we pray? (List specific examples if you can.)

_____

_____

_____

_____

Write. In Exodus 17:8-13 Moses made the connection between prayer and God's power. But as he prayed with his arms raised, he grew weary. He knew better than to drop them to his sides; he had done that and watched his troops get wiped out. So his friends Aaron and Hur held his arms up. What a picture — Moses being supported by caring people who wanted to help him keep the power flowing!

❊   ❊   ❊   ❊

Write about an experience you have had of being supported by others in prayer.

 **Prayer Journal.** Thank God for what you are learning from his Word. Express ways you want to grow in understanding prayer and power.

❖   ❖   ❖   ❖

Write your prayers to God. Raise to him the questions and needs you have as you learn more about prayer. Tell him your fears and concerns.

Record. Skeptics may argue that answered prayers are only coincidences, but as an English archbishop once observed, "It's amazing how many coincidences occur when one begins to pray."

This space is designed for you to keep a list of what you are praying for. Make your list in a column on the left. Then return to the list frequently and note on the right how God responds to your prayer. This list will be a source of praise and comfort to you as you see the ways God is working in your life.

❄   ❄   ❄   ❄

Make a brief list here of what you have talked with God about throughout this chapter.

_____

_____

_____

_____

_____

_____

_____

2

God Is Willing

 **Write.** I had access to anything my father owned, just as soon as I was capable of handling it properly. One of his prized possessions was a forty-five-foot sailboat. When I was in eighth grade, my dad would say to me, "Why don't you get one of your buddies, hike out to South Haven and take the boat out?" Once my brother and I had our driver's licenses, he was equally generous with the car. If he got a new car, the first thing he'd do when he came home was to give us each a set of keys and say, "Take it for a spin. If you want to take it out on a date, go ahead."

❋　❋　❋　❋

Write about a person who has been generous to you. (Consider generosity with time and insights as well as material goods.)

Spend a few moments thanking God for this person and for the impact his or her generosity has had on your life.

Reflect. There are a hundred reasons not to pray:

—God is busy keeping the cosmos in order. He doesn't want to hear about my little problems.

—God would think I was selfish if I prayed for my own needs. If I really love him, I'll put myself last.

—God has important things to do. He's not in the business of taking care of me, and I won't ask him to do it.

❀   ❀   ❀   ❀

What reasons are you likely to give yourself for not praying?

_____

_____

_____

_____

_____

_____

_____

_____

_____

_____

As you review what you have written in your reasons not to pray, what are these reasons saying about your view of God? about your view of yourself?

Study. Most fathers love to be generous with their children. Jesus understood this, and that is why he used fathers to explain God's generosity.

❊ ❊ ❊ ❊

Read Matthew 7:9-11. What picture does this passage provide you of the "table" God provides for his family?

_____

Read Galatians 4:6-7. What do you find here that encourages you to talk to God about your needs?

_____

_____

Read Romans 8:15-17. This passage begins by saying that we do not need to be slaves to fear. Why?

_____

_____

What do you see here that assures you of God's generosity?

_____

_____

Select one of the three passages above and spend ten minutes meditating on it phrase by phrase. What is God revealing to you about himself?

_____

_____

 **Write.** For some reason most of us have a hard time accepting the gifts God gives us. In the past, when God would bless me with a special portion of his Spirit, a material item I had been wanting or a warm new relationship, I can distinctly remember feeling, *God must have had his wires crossed. Why would he do that for me?* In fact, I would feel guilty about my good fortune, as if I had somehow acquired something that God didn't really want me to have.

I'm learning to give God a little credit. If imperfect fathers love to bestow blessings on their children, imagine how our perfect Father in heaven must delight in giving good gifts to us, his beloved children.

Fill this page with a "blessing count." Write down every good thing you can think of that has come to you from the hand of God. Hint: Include opportunities, people, skills, events, as well as "things."

Prayer Journal. Use this space to pray on paper.

Confess to God any reluctance you have about praying. Express your appreciation to God for the bounty he has already given to your life.

❀   ❀   ❀   ❀

Ask and it will be given to you; seek and you will find; knock and the door will be opened to you. For everyone who asks receives; he who seeks finds; and to him who knocks, the door will be opened.
MATTHEW 7:7-8

Express in writing a prayer of desire to God. He invites you to ask.

_____

_____

_____

_____

_____

_____

_____

_____

_____

_____

_____

Record.

Will not God bring about justice for his chosen ones, who cry out to him day and night? . . . I tell you, he will see that they get justice, and quickly.

LUKE 18:7-8

❈   ❈   ❈   ❈

Make a brief list here of what you have talked with God about throughout this chapter.

_____

_____

_____

_____

_____

_____

_____

_____

_____

_____

3

God Is Able

Reflect. I used to make excuses for my faint-hearted prayer life. But God convinced me that I was not being honest with myself. The real reason my prayers were weak was that my faith was weak.

In my head, I have always believed in God's omnipotence. I write about it and preach about it. But too often this belief hasn't registered where it really counts—in my heart. When my heart is not persuaded, I don't pray about difficult situations and ask God to fulfill pressing needs. Somewhere deep down, I don't believe he can do anything about them.

What are some pressing needs that you find difficult to pray about? (Consider marriage, work, faith, children, health.) List them here. Make a note next to each item that suggests why you hesitate to pray about that particular subject.

Need   **I Hesitate to Pray Because . . .**

Talk to God about what you are learning from your list.

 **Write.** God is capable of handling any problem we could bring him. Creating planets isn't much of a problem for him. Neither is raising the dead.

How have you seen God's power at work? Consider your own personal past, your observation of God's work in the lives of others, incidents recorded in Scripture.

❋ ❋ ❋ ❋

I have seen God's power over nature . . .

_____

_____

_____

_____

_____

_____

_____

_____

_____

_____

I have seen God's power over circumstances . . .

I have seen God's power over human hearts . . .

 **Study**. *God's Power over Nature*
Read Matthew 14:22-36. What examples do you
see here of God's power?

In verse 31, Jesus says to Peter, "You of little faith, . . . why
did you doubt?" In what ways do you think Peter would see
Jesus differently after this event?

God's Power over Circumstances
Read 1 Kings 18:1-39. What circumstances were against Elijah?

In verse 39, at the closing of this sequence of events, we see
all the people prostrate on the ground crying, "The LORD—
he is God! The LORD—he is God." How did God bring
about this change?

God's Power over Hearts
Read Acts 9:1-31. Describe Saul's "heart" as you see it at the opening of this account.

_____

_____

_____

_____

What evidences do you see of a changed heart by verse 31?

_____

_____

_____

How does this story impact the way you might pray for a person who is not yet a Christian?

_____

_____

_____

_____

 **Prayer Journal.** A "prayer warrior" is a person who is convinced that God is omnipotent—that God has the power to do anything, to change anyone and to intervene in any circumstance. A person who truly believes this refuses to doubt God.

Hang back no longer! God, through Christ, has issued you a personal invitation to call on him anytime. In fact, it is impossible to come into his presence uninvited, because his Word tells us to "pray continually" (1 Thessalonians 5:17).

❊ ❊ ❊ ❊

Look back at page 23, where you reflected on needs that are hard for you to pray about. Choose one need that is particularly troublesome to you right now. Write a prayer below, expressing your desires in this area. Be brave enough to ask God to meet those needs—providing what he knows is best.

Page back through this chapter of your journal to review all that you have written about God's character. Write a prayer of praise to him in the space below. Be sure to include your own responses to these qualities of God's nature.

Record.

Now to him who is able to do immeasurably more than all we ask or imagine, according to his power that is at work within us, to him be glory in the church and in Christ Jesus throughout all generations, for ever and ever! Amen.

EPHESIANS 3:20-21

❈   ❈   ❈   ❈

Make a brief list here of what you have talked with God about throughout this chapter.

4

Heart-Building Habits

 **Reflect.** Our habits of prayer often follow our natural bent. So here are two warnings. The first is for those who love lists and formulas. You already practice a rigorous spiritual regimen. Before you dutifully lengthen your list of spiritual duties, back off. Do you need to weigh your-self further down—or to bring your heavy load to Jesus?

My second warning is for those who make the equal and opposite error. You are thinking, *I don't need any structure or rigorous habits to make my heart grow. I go with the spiritual flow. I'll just see what happens.* You would benefit from adding some structure to your spiritual life to ensure that you get time with God.

❊   ❊   ❊   ❊

Which of the two descriptions above is closest to your patterns?

What is good about your current patterns of prayer?

What weakness or dangers do you suspect might come from your current habits of prayer?

Write. Jesus invites us to pray regularly, privately, sincerely, and specifically. Use these pages to evaluate your current habits in each area and to set goals or ideals for future practice.

❀　❀　❀　❀

Pray Regularly

Describe your current habits of prayer. Be specific and honest. How often have you prayed in the past month? How regularly? Under what circumstances?

What would you like your habits of regular prayer to become? (Be specific. How often? When? Where?)

Pray Privately

Where do you pray? How do you guard against distraction and interruption? What is your ratio between public and private prayer?

What are some goals to ensure quality private time with God?

Pray Sincerely

How honest are you with God? If you use liturgical prayers, are you able to say them with your whole heart? Are your public prayers *honest?* Do you consciously pray when you sing hymns or songs that are actually prayers?

What goals can you set to gain honesty in prayer?

Pray Specifically

What is your current habit regarding specific prayer?

How can you improve in this area?

 **Study.** *Read Matthew 6:5-8.* Three times in this passage Jesus says "Do not." What are we not to do? Why?

What do the reasons behind each "do not" tell you about God's design for prayer?

What are we to do instead of the "do nots"? Why?

How can the kind of private prayer described here keep our public prayers from becoming hypocritical?

Would you say that you pray *better* in public or in private?

What does your answer reveal about your values and motives?

Read Christ's model prayer as it is recorded in Matthew 6:9-13. What major areas does Jesus cover in his prayer?

In practical terms, what does each of these areas illustrate?

What attitudes toward God the Father do you detect in this prayer?

If you were to pray in the same manner as this prayer, how and what would you pray?

Prayer Journal. Use Christ's model prayer as a pattern for your own praying. Meditate on each phrase, then write in specific terms what you want to say to God from in that area.

❀   ❀   ❀   ❀

Our Father in heaven,

hallowed be your name,

your kingdom come,

your will be done

on earth as it is in heaven.

Give us this day our daily bread.

Forgive us our debts,

---

as we forgive our debtors.

And lead us not into temptation,

---

but deliver us from the evil one.

Record.

But when you pray, go into your room, close the door and pray to your Father, who is unseen. Then your Father, who sees what is done in secret, will reward you.

MATTHEW 6:6

❊   ❊   ❊   ❊

Make a brief list here of what you have talked with God about throughout this chapter.

5

Praying Like Jesus

Write. Describe one of your best memories of prayer. What was the time, place, event, circumstance? What did you do? How were you aware of God's presence? In what ways were you changed because of this experience?

❊   ❊   ❊   ❊

 **Reflect.** I was moving fast, always on the go but never looking deeply inside. I never did the kind of reflection that leads to growth. And I was paying the price—committing the same stupid sins over and over, living with the same heavy load of guilt.

So I made a difficult decision. I decided that each day I would try to honestly assess my soul's condition. I would look inside myself, and I would write down what I saw. Feeling awkward and embarrassed, I took out a spiral notebook and started to write. "God, here are some frustrations in my life. They aren't going away, so I might as well take a look at them." Or, "Here's a relationship I'm concerned about. It's not good, and I don't know how to improve it." Or, "Here are some blessings you've poured into my life." After writing a paragraph or two, I would reflect on what I had written.

❈　❈　❈　❈

How is *your* soul? Examine yourself and write your observations on these two pages.

 **Study.** Psalm 62:8 says, "Pour out your hearts to him." We can talk to God. We can say, "Lord, this is how I feel today. I've been thinking about this recently. I'm worried about this. I'm depressed about that. I'm happy about this."

❊   ❊   ❊   ❊

Read all of Psalm 62. In this prayer psalm, David weaves back and forth between his current circumstances and what he knows to be true about God. What are these circumstances (vv. 3-4, 9-10)?

What does David know about God (vv. 1-2, 5-8, 11-12)?

How do these characteristics of God impact David?

How do the same qualities of God help you deal with your own circumstances?

Pray phrases of this psalm, praising God for who he is.

Write. I created a "prayer room" near the credenza in a corner of my former office. In my prayer place I put an open Bible, a sign that says, "God is able," a crown of thorns to remind me of the suffering Savior, and a shepherd's staff that I often hold up while making requests.

That office became a holy place for me. I arrived there around six o'clock in the morning, when no one was around and the phone was unlikely to ring, and there I communed with the Lord. I poured out my heart to him, worshiped him, prayed for members of my congregation and received remarkable answers to prayer.

My office has since been relocated, and I now have a new prayer corner. But I have warm memories of the old one — not because there is anything holy about the corner itself but because of what happened there.

❈   ❈   ❈   ❈

What time and place could you use regularly for prayer?

What visual aids could help you worship?

Prayer Journal. God-honoring prayers are not simply shopping lists. They are more than cries for help, strength, mercy and miracles. Authentic prayer should include worship: "Our Father in heaven, hallowed be your name" (Matthew 6:9). It should include submission: "Your will be done on earth as it is in heaven" (v. 10). Requests are certainly appropriate: "Give us today our daily bread" (v. 11); so are confessions: "Forgive us our debts, as we also forgive our debtors" (v. 12).

❧　❧　❧　❧

Record your prayer of today on these two pages. Use the four areas Jesus outlined in his model prayer: worship, submission, requests, confession.

It's been nearly fifteen years since I started writing reflections about my day. I soon began writing out my whole prayer and reading it back to God. I've been blessed in many ways because of this discipline. It helps me concentrate. I used to get no further than "Dear God" and I'd already be thinking of the person I was meeting for lunch, or the board meeting agenda, or what my family would be doing after dinner. When I'm moving a pen across paper, it is much easier to keep focused. Writing also forces me to be specific; broad generalities don't look good on paper. And it helps me see when God answers prayers.

Record.

Trust in him at all times, O people;
pour out your hearts to him,
for God is our refuge.

PSALM 62:8

❀   ❀   ❀   ❀

Make a brief list here of what you have talked with God
about throughout this chapter.

6

A Pattern for Prayer

Reflect. Developing prayer fitness is like developing physical fitness: we need a pattern to avoid becoming imbalanced. Without a routine, we will probably fall into the "Please God" trap: "Please God, give me. Please God, help me. Please God, cover me. Please God, arrange this."

I can tell you from personal experience where imbalanced prayer leads. Sensing the carelessness and one-sidedness of our prayers, we begin to feel guilty about praying. Guilt leads to faint-heartedness, and that in turn leads to prayerlessness. When praying makes us feel guilty, pretty soon we stop praying.

If that has happened to you, it's time to set up a prayer routine.

❊   ❊   ❊   ❊

What routines or patterns of prayer have you used in the past?

Whether or not you have used a routine for prayer, what value can you see to a regular pattern of praying?

 **Study.** I am going to offer you a pattern to follow. It's not the only pattern or the perfect pattern, but it's a good pattern that has been used for many years in Christian circles. It's balanced, and it's easy to use. All you have to remember is the word *ACTS*, an acrostic whose four letters stand for *adoration, confession, thanksgiving* and *supplication*.

❀ ❀ ❀ ❀

Read Psalm 148. How can this psalm help you express *adoration* to God?

_____

_____

Read Psalm 103:8-13. Why might these verses inspire you to make *confession* to God?

_____

_____

Read Luke 17:11-19. What do you see of yourself in this story of *thanksgiving?*

_____

_____

Read James 1:5. How might this verse assure you that it is all right to make *supplication* to God?

_____

_____

 **Reflect.** Page through a hymnal or songbook. Or choose from this list of praise-ful Scripture passages: Psalm 8, 19, 23, 46, 95, 100; Luke 1:46-55, 68-79; Ephesians 1:3-14. Among these, find a song, hymn or passage of Scripture that prepares you to worship God. Copy it in the space below. Then read or sing it to God.

✻ ✻ ✻ ✻

Prayer Journal. I've found the ACTS formula especially helpful when I write out my prayers. Starting with *adoration*, I might write something like this: "Good morning, Lord! I feel free to praise you today, and I'm choosing this moment when I'm fresh and ready, willing and able to get going, to stop and say that I love you. You are a wonderful God. Your personality and character bring me to my knees. You are holy, just, righteous, gracious, merciful, fair, tender, loving, fatherly and forgiving. I'm thrilled to be in relationship with you today, and I worship you now."

❋ ❋ ❋ ❋

Write your own prayer of *adoration* in the space below.

After adoration I move to *confession*. I might write: "Please forgive me for committing the sin of partiality. It is so much easier for me to direct my love and attention toward those who seem to 'have it all together.' Without even realizing it, I find myself avoiding troubled people. I'm sorry. Thanks for your impartiality to me. Please forgive me, and now I claim your forgiveness." Then I take my pen and cross out what I've written, saying, "I thank you that I'm free from this. I'm glad the slate is clean. Thank you for forgiving me."

❁ ❁ ❁ ❁

Write your own prayer of *confession* in the space below.

Thanksgiving is easy for me. I thank God for specific answers to prayer, for helping me in my work, for people's responsiveness, for protecting our elders and staff and board, for material and relational blessings and for anything else that makes me particularly happy. Thanking the Lord every day keeps me from being covetous, and putting my thanks on paper reminds me of the incredible number of blessings I enjoy.

❀　❀　❀　❀

Write your own prayer of *thanksgiving* in the space below.

I'm glad that *supplication* is last. Once I've worshiped God, confessed my sins and given thanks, it's okay for me to take out my shopping list. In fact, James 4:2 says, "You do not have, because you do not ask God." I used to be vague about what I needed. "Please help me and cover me and keep me out of trouble." I don't do that anymore. I list specific requests, leave them with God and regularly review them to see how he has answered me.

❀   ❀   ❀   ❀

Write your own prayer of *supplication* in the space below.

Record.

"Worthy is the Lamb, who was slain,
to receive power and wealth and wisdom and strength
and honor and glory and praise! . . .
To him who sits on the throne and to the Lamb
be praise and honor and glory and power,
for ever and ever!

R E V E L A T I O N 5:12-13

❃　❃　❃　❃

Make a brief list here of what you have talked with God
about throughout this chapter.

7

Mountain-Moving Prayer

Reflect.

Jesus replied, "I tell you the truth, if you have faith and do not doubt, . . . you can say to this mountain, 'Go, throw yourself into the sea,' and it will be done. If you believe, you will receive whatever you ask for in prayer."
MATTHEW 21:21-22

According to the Bible, believers can be confident that their prayers will be answered. Our prayers are more than wishes, hopes or feeble aspirations—but only if we pray with believing, faith-filled hearts. That is the kind of prayer that moves mountains.

Probably every human being alive is standing in the shadow of at least one mountain that just will not move: a destructive habit, a character flaw, an impossible marriage or work situation, a financial problem, a physical disability.

❀ ❀ ❀ ❀

What is your current personal "mountain"?

Why does this feel like a mountain to you?

 **Write.** Use these two pages to make a sketch or drawing of your mountain. Sketch in symbols or words for the obstacles that make your mountain seem insurmountable. Make a cartoon figure of yourself in that picture.

After you have finished the sketch of your mountain, surround your mountain at regular intervals with written descriptions of God. For example: *God is good, God has all power, God loves me.*

 **Study.** God gives us faith as we walk with him. Joshua 3 illustrates this principle. The Israelites are camped on the bank of the Jordan River. Forty years earlier, they miraculously escaped from Egypt. For a generation, they have been wandering in a rugged wilderness, all their needs miraculously met by God. Now they are in sight of the Promised Land, but they have an enormous problem: a river is right in their path.

❖   ❖   ❖   ❖

Read Joshua 3:1 — 4:7. Why would the people of Israel think crossing the Jordan would be difficult or even impossible?

What preparations did they make to cross the river into the land God had promised to give them (3:1-6)?

What did Joshua do to reassure the people of God's presence and his power (3:7-13)?

How did the priests show spiritual leadership (3:14-17)?

In what ways would the twelve stones help future generations to remember what God had done (4:1-7)?

Write. Sometimes when we face a "mountain" (or a flooded river), it helps to remember what God has done for us in the past. Joshua's stones, taken from the bottom of a miraculously dry riverbed, were solid reminders of God's care for his people.

Search your memory for pictures of God's past work in your life. What "stones" do you see? Draw or write this story of God at work in your past. Consider how these "stones" might give you courage to tackle the mountain you drew on pages 56-57.

❊   ❊   ❊   ❊

Prayer Journal. The first principle for moving a mountain is this: *Faith comes from looking at God, not at the mountain.*

❧   ❧   ❧   ❧

Look back at the picture you drew of your mountain, along with the descriptions of God with which you surrounded that mountain. Write a prayer that incorporates what you drew, but focus primarily on the character of God.

The second principle of mountain-moving faith is this: *God gives us faith as we walk with him.*

Just as the priests of Israel, carrying God's ark, had to first set their feet into a flooded river, God may expect you to begin some steps with him to conquer your mountain. Prayerfully consider this, asking God what he expects of you in this situation. Record your prayer here, along with any steps that you ought to be taking.

Record.

Great is thy faithfulness! Great is thy faithfulness!
Morning by morning new mercies I see;
All I have needed thy hand hath provided —
Great is thy faithfulness, Lord, unto me!
"Great Is Thy Faithfulness"

❀　❀　❀　❀

Make a brief list here of what you have talked with God about throughout this chapter.

8

The Hurt of Unanswered Prayer

Reflect. Nearly every week someone meets me at the church or calls my office and asks, "Bill, didn't Jesus say, 'Ask and it will be given to you; seek and you will find; knock and the door will be opened to you'?" I couldn't begin to count how many people I've counseled about the mystery—or perhaps more accurately, the agony—of unanswered prayer. And the people who suffer most keenly are those who truly believe that prayer moves mountain.

❀　❀　❀　❀

What have you been praying about that you fear God is not answering?

_____

_____

_____

_____

_____

_____

_____

 **Study.** Sometimes God says no. Study each of the three events below and note why God said no in each case.

❀ ❀ ❀ ❀

Luke 9:51-56

_____

_____

_____

_____

Mark 10:35-45

_____

_____

_____

_____

Luke 9:28-36

_____

_____

_____

_____

 **Write.** If the disciples were capable of making wrong requests—requests that were totally self-serving, patently materialistic, short-sighted, immature—so am I and so are you. Fortunately, our God loves us too much to say yes to inappropriate requests. He will answer such prayers, but he will say no. I wouldn't want a God who would do any less than that.

❖ ❖ ❖ ❖

When has God said no or "not now" to one of your requests and you have later been relieved that he did not grant what you asked? Write of this event on the next couple of pages as if it were a story.

_____

_____

_____

_____

_____

_____

_____

_____

Prayer Journal. Sometimes the reason for our request is not wrong, but in the infinite mystery of things, the outcome still seems to be no. Every day, godly people are stricken with dreaded deadly diseases. Praying parents die without having seen their wayward children return to the fold. Why would an all-loving, all-powerful God deny valid requests from faithful believers?

❈　❈　❈　❈

We can't always know *why* God does not choose to answer our prayers in the way that we want. But it is all right to talk with him about our frustrations in that area. Use the rest of this page to write a prayer that expresses your yearnings over requests that you have made but he has not granted.

 **Prayer Journal.** Use the ACTS method you learned in chapter six to write out your prayers. Allow the important steps of adoration, confession and thanksgiving to draw you close to God even as you are struggling with the question of how God answers prayer.

❊　❊　❊　❊

Write your own prayer of *adoration* in the space below.

_____

_____

_____

_____

_____

Write your own prayer of *confession* in the space below.

_____

_____

_____

_____

_____

Write your own prayer of *thanksgiving* in the space below.

Write your own prayer of *supplication* in the space below.

 **Record.**

"For my thoughts are not your thoughts,
  neither are your ways my ways," declares the LORD.
"As the heavens are higher than the earth,
  so are my ways higher than your ways
  and my thoughts than your thoughts."

I S A I A H 55:8-9

❈   ❈   ❈   ❈

Make a brief list here of what you have talked with God
about throughout this chapter.

9

Prayer Busters

 **Reflect.** If someone asked you what most motivates you to develop your personal prayer life, how would you answer? What drives you to your knees and makes you want to pray more? What makes your prayers more fervent?

Answered prayer really motivates me. It makes me feel like Moses on the mountain with his arms upraised, directing the battle through his prayers. When my prayers have that kind of demonstrable results, it's fun to pray.

❀　　❀　　❀　　❀

What experiences have you had with answered prayers in your past?

_____

_____

_____

To what extent have you seen God respond to your recent prayers?

_____

_____

_____

 **Study.** In the last chapter we looked at two major reasons prayers go unanswered: the request may be inappropriate, and the timing may be off. In this chapter we look at a third reason for unanswered prayer: there may be a problem in the life of the person who is praying.

I call these reasons *prayer busters.*

❄   ❄   ❄   ❄

Study each of the six passages below, making appropriate notes. What reason does each suggest for unanswered prayer? What other helpful information can you find in or around the passage?

James 4:2

_____

_____

_____

Isaiah 59:2

_____

_____

_____

Matthew 5:23-24

_____

_____

_____

James 4:3

_____

_____

_____

_____

Proverbs 21:13

_____

_____

_____

_____

James 1:5-8

_____

_____

_____

_____

_____

 **Write.** If you are faced with a long list of unanswered prayers, you may want to pay special attention to this third category of reasons that God may not answer prayer. It is unlikely that all your requests are inappropriate, even though some may very well be. It's unlikely that your timing is always off, even though sometimes you may push ahead of God. It's more likely that some malfunction in your life is blocking your prayers, even the appropriate, well-timed ones.

❊　❊　❊　❊

On these two pages is a list of each of the six "prayer busters" found in the *study* section. Make an honest search of your mind and heart for ways that you may have fallen into one or more of these patterns. Write down specific examples.

Prayerlessness

_____

_____

_____

_____

Unconfessed Sin

_____

_____

_____

_____

Broken Relationships

_____

_____

_____

Selfishness

_____

_____

_____

Uncaring Attitudes

_____

_____

_____

Inadequate Faith

_____

_____

_____

Prayer Journal.

Search me, O God, and know my heart;
test me and know my anxious thoughts.
See if there is any offensive way in me,
and lead me in the way everlasting.

P S A L M 139:23-24

❈   ❈   ❈   ❈

The "prayer of examen" is a step beyond taking a look inside and confessing our sin. In the prayer of examen, we invite God to take that look with us; we open the dusty corners of our souls and say, "Lord, search me." David made that request at the close of his glorious prayer psalm, Psalm 139.

You can invite God to do the same as you continue to search out potential flaws within yourself that might result in unanswered prayer. Use these two pages to record your prayers. If you are able, begin and end your prayer of examen with David's words from the psalm, quoted above.

Record.

He has told you, O mortal, what is good;
*   and what does the LORD require of you*
*   but to do justice, and to love kindness,*
*   and to walk humbly with your God?*

M I C A H 6:8 NRSV

❀ ❀ ❀ ❀

Make a brief list here of what you have talked with God about throughout this chapter.

10

Cooling Off On Prayer

 **Reflect.** When I look back over twenty-five years of spiritual life, I see certain seasons when I prayed eagerly and often. I was filled with joy and the anticipation of God's blessings. Supernatural things happened in my life, in the lives of people I prayed for and in the church.

And then, for who knows what reason, my prayer life would begin to wind down until I had almost given up praying. I would still pray at meals and at church functions, of course, but not a whole lot more than that. Prayer would seem pointless. This prayerless season could last for weeks or even months.

❀　❀　❀　❀

Which paragraph above is closest to your current prayer life?

What is satisfying about prayer in your current stage of spiritual development?

What is difficult about prayer at your current stage?

 **Write.** If your praying is running cool just now, there are three obvious areas to check. These will not ferret out all causes of lukewarm prayer, but they catch enough problems to be worthy of serious consideration.

❀   ❀   ❀   ❀

First, evaluate in writing your current *daily rhythm* of prayer. If this is less than satisfactory, consider (also in writing) whether you can connect your time of prayer to some activity that you do every day.

Second, evaluate your *place* of prayer. Any place can become a place of prayer, but the people I know who pray fervently and joyfully and consistently can usually describe the physical environment in which they pray daily. Would a different place lead to more fervent praying?

Third, consider whether the problem with prayer is not a lack of time or place, but a *lack of eagerness*. If that describes our feelings, we may be suffering from guilt of shame. Something we have done—or are currently doing—may be standing between us and God. Sometimes when I'm trying to help someone understand why they don't pray anymore, I say, "Let's just backtrack. Do you know when you started feeling this way? What else was happening in your life at that time?"

If you sense that your praying is cool or indifferent, try the exercise above. Write your observations in this space.

Did your writing reveal something that may be sin? Old-fashioned sin is strong enough to create an ever-widening gap in our relationship with God. The wider the gap, the less likely we are to pray. And the less we pray, the wider the gap becomes.

The good news is that you can come back into fellowship with the Father right now. You can say a prayer of repentance like this: "God, I'm sorry for _____. Please forgive me. I want to turn from this, and I want to come back into relationship with you."

 **Prayer Journal.** Perhaps you have done all the right things. You have made room for prayer in your daily schedule, and you are unaware of any sin coming between you and God. All the same, you know you are drifting away from him. You are about to give up on prayer, because you are discouraged. Disillusioned. Or even despairing. Some things will never be clear this side of eternity. "We live by faith," says the apostle Paul, "not by sight" (2 Corinthians 5:7).

❖   ❖   ❖   ❖

Are you disappointed by unanswered prayer? If so, write a prayer expressing your disappointment to God. If it is possible to do so honestly, express also your desire to continue to live by faith.

 **Study.** *Read* the story Jesus told his disciples in *Luke 18:1-8.*

❁   ❁   ❁   ❁

What was the widow's request?

_____

_____

What phrases in the text help you know the character of the judge?

_____

_____

How was this judge different from God?

_____

_____

Why was the woman successful?

_____

_____

Why did Jesus tell his disciples this story?

_____

_____

How might this story bring you hope about praying?

_____

_____

 **Prayer Journal.** Some years ago we had a baptism Sunday, and many people became Christ's followers. I thought my heart would explode for joy. Afterward, in the stairwell, I bumped into a woman who was crying. I couldn't understand how anyone could weep after such a celebration, so I stopped and asked her if she was all right.

"I'm crying," the woman replied, "because I came this close—*this* close—to giving up on her. I mean, after five years I said, *Who needs this? God isn't listening.* After ten years, I said, *Why am I wasting my breath?* After fifteen years I said, *This is absurd.* After nineteen years I said, *I'm just a fool.* But I guess I just kept praying, even though my faith was weak. I kept praying, and she gave her life to Christ, and she was baptized today."

The woman paused and looked me in the eye. "I will never doubt the power of prayer again," she said.

❉   ❉   ❉   ❉

Have you almost given up on some particular subject of prayer? Use the space here to pray again—as persistently and as eloquently as you can.

_____

_____

_____

_____

_____

_____

Record.

Then Jesus told ... them that they should always pray and not give up.... And will not God bring about justice for his chosen ones, who cry out to him day and night? Will he keep putting them off? I tell you, he will see that they get justice, and quickly.
LUKE 18:1, 7-8

❀   ❀   ❀   ❀

Make a brief list here of what you have talked with God about throughout this chapter.

_____

_____

_____

_____

_____

_____

_____

_____

_____

11

Slowing Down to Pray

 **Reflect.** Cram it in. Start earlier. Work later. Take work home. Use a laptop on the commuter train. Phone clients while you drive. Check your e-mail while you fly. Schedule breakfasts, lunches and dinners for profit. Getting caught up in that intense pace can be rewarding! It's exciting when the adrenaline starts to flow and you get on a roll, when your motor starts racing faster and faster.

But you don't have to be in business to be overcommitted. Homemakers with small children know what it means to do ten thousand rpms all day long. Almost every minute of every day is consumed by those little creatures who pull on your pant legs, color on your walls, track mud on your carpet, throw food on your floor and then have the audacity to fuss in the middle of the night. And the pace of single working parents is double or triple that of the rest of us.

❋ ❋ ❋ ❋

Reflect on the busiest time of your life. What activities filled your days and nights?

Describe your patterns of praying during that intensely busy time.

How does that era compare with your current patterns of prayer and spiritual reflection?

 **Study.** Looking at how we function at top speed without time for reflection, I ask myself, *Where does the still, small voice of God fit into our hectic lives? When do we allow him to lead us? And if this seldom or never happens, how can we lead truly authentic Christian lives?*

Authentic Christians stand apart from others. Their character seems deeper, their ideas fresher, their spirit softer.

❊   ❊   ❊   ❊

Read Psalm 1:1-6 for a picture of an authentic Christian. What contrasts do you see between the person described in verses 1-3 and the person described in verses 4-6?

Consider an authentic Christian whom you admire. In what ways is that person like the tree described in verse 3?

What do verses 2-3 suggest about the way the person described here uses time?

What warnings does this psalm contain that would encourage you to follow this pattern?

What have you enjoyed about your own "treelike" experiences with God?

 **Write.** Authentic Christians are willing to slow down and look inside. Most of us, says Gordon MacDonald in *Ordering Your Private World*, live unexamined lives. We repeat the same errors day after day. We don't learn much from the decisions we make, whether they are good or bad. We don't know why we're here or where we're going. One benefit of journaling is to force us to examine our lives.

❄   ❄   ❄   ❄

Go to a drugstore, says MacDonald, and buy a spiral notebook. Plan to write in this notebook every day, but restrict yourself to one page. Every day when you open to the next blank sheet of paper, write the same first word: *Yesterday.* Follow this with a paragraph or two recounting yesterday's events, sort of a postgame analysis.

Write whatever you want—perhaps a little description of the people you interacted with, your appointments, decisions, thoughts, feelings, high points, low points, frustrations, what you read in your Bible, what you were going to do and didn't. According to MacDonald, this exercise causes a tremendous step forward in spiritual development.

Yesterday . . .

Prayer Journal. After journaling has reduced my rpms from ten thousand to five thousand, I flip all the way to the back of my spiral notebook and write a prayer. As with the journal, I limit my writing to one page. This keeps the exercise from overwhelming me and ensures that I do it every day. It also takes a realistic amount of time, given the other responsibilities I face daily.

Once I write out the prayer, I put the notebook on my credenza and kneel down. Not everyone is like me in this respect, but I find I pray much more effectively on my knees. I read the prayer aloud, adding other comments or concerns as I go along.

❄ ❄ ❄ ❄

Use the next page to do your own praying.

*The archenemy of spiritual
authenticity is busyness.*

Reflect.

"Be still and know that I am God;
 I will be exalted among the nations,
 I will be exalted in the earth."
The LORD Almighty is with us;
 the God of Jacob is our fortress.
P S A L M 46:10-11

❄   ❄   ❄   ❄

Make a brief list here of what you have talked with God
about throughout this chapter.

12

The Importance of Listening

**Reflect.** It's ironic that most of the time we think of prayer as talking to God, rarely stopping to wonder whether God might want to talk to us. But as I've studied prayer and prayed, I've sensed God saying, "If we enjoy a relationship, why are you doing all the talking? Let me get a word in somewhere!"

❀   ❀   ❀   ❀

Reflect on a time that you were able to listen to God. (Consider his communication through Scripture, through his people and through direct leading of the Holy Spirit.) How did you respond? What came of this experience?

_____

_____

_____

_____

_____

_____

Write. Which paragraph on these pages is closest to your own approach to listening to God? Study each approach, then write your observations about the strengths and dangers of each, including how you relate to God in these ways.

❋   ❋   ❋   ❋

Once a person turns his or her life over to Jesus Christ, it is no longer business as usual. Life no longer consists only of that which can be seen or smelled or felt or figured out by human logic. It includes walking by faith, and that means opening oneself to the miraculous ministry of the Holy Spirit. We may know some Christians who claim to be doing this, but they have performed a kind of intellectual lobotomy on themselves, and they expect the Holy Spirit to choose their socks in the morning, their restaurant for lunch and their crossword puzzle in the evening. They claim to experience a leading an hour, a vision a day, a miracle a week.

Other Christians are twentieth-century rationalists. To them the Holy Spirit's promptings seem to go against human nature and conventional thought patterns. Accustomed to walking by sight, steering their own ships and making unilateral decisions, they are squeamish about letting the Holy Spirit begin his supernatural ministry in their lives. They wish the package were a little neater. They would like his ministry to be quantified and described. The Holy Spirit seems elusive and mysterious, and that unnerves them.

 **Study.** A two-way conversation between a mortal human being and the infinite God would certainly be supernatural—but what's so surprising about that? The normal Christian life has a supernatural dimension. As the apostle Paul says in 2 Corinthians 5:7, "We live by faith, not by sight." Listening to God speak to us through his Holy Spirit is not only normal; it is essential.

✿　✿　✿　✿

Study each passage listed on these two pages. Below each reference write observations that answer this question: What can you learn about listening to God from this passage?

Genesis 3:8-9

John 6:44-45

John 14:15-18

John 16:13-15

Romans 8:1-17

Galatians 5:16-26

Prayer Journal.

If you love me, you will obey what I command. And I will ask the Father, and he will give you another Counselor to be with you forever—the Spirit of truth. The world cannot accept him, because it neither sees him nor knows him. But you know him, for he lives with you and will be in you. I will not leave you as orphans.

J O H N 14:15-18

❀ ❀ ❀ ❀

Pray over and reflect on the Scripture above and write your response to God.

Spend five or ten minutes listening to God through the passage you have meditated on and also as a possible response to your written prayer. After this time of silence, record notes about what God may be saying to you.

Record.

But when he, the Spirit of truth, comes, he will guide you in into all truth.

J O H N 16:13

❅   ❅   ❅   ❅

Make a brief list here of what you have talked with God about throughout this chapter.

_____

_____

_____

_____

_____

_____

_____

_____

_____

_____

_____

13

How to Hear God's Leadings

Prayer Journal.
Worship the LORD with gladness;
come before him with joyful songs.
P S A L M   100:2

❖   ❖   ❖   ❖

Worship God with song—whether spoken or sung. Page through a hymnal, songbook or the texts of tapes and CDs. Find one or more that expresses what you would like to say to God and also that prepares you to listen to him. You may want to copy the words on this page. Sing or read aloud your worship to God. After a time of oral praise, write a prayer of praise. Read it aloud to God.

 **Reflect.** No one can become an authentic Christian on a steady diet of activity. Power comes out of stillness; strength comes out of solitude. Decisions that change the entire course of your life come out of the Holy of Holies, your times of stillness before God.

Practice a time of stillness in God's presence. It may help to focus your mind on a particular attribute of God or on a portion of Scripture that praises God. As you engage in this time of silence, pencil notes about whatever pops into your head. When your mind strays away from God, try to draw it back to him keeping pencil notes of your efforts. After fifteen minutes, evaluate your process on the next page.

What do your notes suggest that you need to do in order to quiet your mind in God's presence?

If you accept my words
and store up my commands within you,
turning your ear to wisdom
and applying your heart to understanding,
and if you call out for insight
and cry aloud for understanding,
and if you look for it as for silver
and search for it as for hidden treasure,
then you will understand the fear of the LORD
and find the knowledge of God.

PROVERBS 2:1-5

 **Study.** Does God speak in an audible voice? Some people say they hear him speak. I never have. To me, God speaks by moving in my spirit, by giving me impressions so real that I often write them down. More than once I've sensed God saying to me, "Trust me! Relax in my love." Samuel's story is much more dramatic.

❈ ❈ ❈ ❈

Read 1 Samuel 3:1-21.

What does the passage tell us about the character of Samuel and of Eli?

Why was Samuel confused about the voice he heard?

How did Eli prepare Samuel to be receptive to God?

Why might Samuel have wanted to keep God's message to himself?

How did Eli show his trust in God?

How did the people of Israel benefit from Samuel's pattern of listening to God?

Write. What do you hope (or fear) would happen if you said to God the words of Samuel, "Speak, LORD, for your servant is listening"?

❀ ❀ ❀ ❀

 **Prayer Journal.** When you listen to God, the important thing is not to follow a particular method but to find a way that works for you. Custom design an approach that will still your racing mind and body, soften your heart and enable you to hear God's still, small voice. Then, when you are centered and focused on God, invite him to speak to you. I ask him to speak to me in specific areas. Try using these questions in your own listening to God. Set aside a time of silence. Make notes as you speak and "hear." As you become more practiced in this, you will develop your own series of questions.

❈ ❈ ❈ ❈

What's the next step in developing my character?

What is the next step in my family?

What is the next step in my work?

What is the next step in my relationship with God?

What is the next step in my vocation or education?

What direction should my love relationship go?

What should I do for my parents or children?

How should I plan my times of service, my financial giving?

Record.

Speak, *LORD, for your servant is listening.*
1 SAMUEL 3:9

❈   ❈   ❈   ❈

Make a brief list here of what you have talked with God about throughout this chapter.

14

What to Do with Leadings

Reflect. I was once attending a conference in Southern California. For some strange reason in the middle of one afternoon, I felt I ought to attend a workshop in which I had very little interest. The workshop was in a different building, and as I was walking to it, I met a young man and started talking with him. I was impressed by his tender spirit, and I realized God was knitting out hearts together. Over the course of several months, we corresponded and then visited one another. Eventually he joined our church staff.

I could tell you story after story of leadings God has entrusted to me and to others. I could describe the dramatic effects of obeying God's leadings—or of ignoring them. But such stories may not be to the point. The real question is this: What are you going to do about the leadings *you* receive?

❊　❊　❊　❊

What have you done in the past with leadings that may be from God?

_____

_____

What would you like to do?

_____

_____

Write. Write about a time when you or a friend felt led by God, and later that sense of God's leading proved valid.

Write about a time when you or a friend felt led by God, but this later proved to be an error.

What warning signs might have turned you or your friend away from this action?

Study. What warnings can you pick up from each passage below about potentially false leadings?

❀   ❀   ❀   ❀

Genesis 3:1-7

_____

_____

_____

2 Corinthians 11:14-15

_____

_____

_____

1 Timothy 4:1

_____

_____

_____

_____

John 4:1-3

_____

_____

_____

Study the passages below. How can each passage help you discern a true leading of God?

※　※　※　※

Acts 20:22-24

_____

_____

_____

Ephesians 6:10-18

_____

_____

_____

2 Timothy 2:22

_____

_____

_____

James 4:7

_____

_____

_____

Prayer Journal. We can summarize that a leading is probably from God if has three characteristics. (1) God's leading will be consistent with his Word. (2) God's leading will be consistent with who he made you to be. (3) God's leading often requires some sacrifice or steps of faith.

❀   ❀   ❀   ❀

In prayer, bring to God a decision that you must make. Ask for his leading, keeping in mind the criteria listed above. Record your prayer and any sense of God's leading in the space here.

Let me add a few cautions about leadings that we think come from God. I'm not saying you should automatically reject such leadings unless they are also against Scripture, but reconsider them and treat them carefully.

❋ If a leading requires you to make a major, life-changing decision in a short period of time, question it.

❋ If a leading requires you to go deeply into debt or place someone else in a position of awkwardness, compromise or danger, question it.

❋ If a leading requires you to shatter family relationships or important friendships, question it.

❋ If a leading creates unrest in the spirit of mature Christian friends or counselors as you share it with them, question it.

If you felt a leading as you prayed earlier, test it against these criteria as well.

Do you have a friend or family member who is drifting toward one of these danger areas? Devote this space to prayer for that person, asking for God's genuine leading in his or her life.

Record.

And now, compelled by the Spirit, I am going to Jerusalem, not knowing what will happen to me there. . . . However, I consider my life worth nothing to me, if only I may finish the race and complete the task the Lord Jesus has given me — the task of testifying to the gospel of God's grace.

A C T S 20:22, 24

❀ ❀ ❀ ❀

Make a brief list here of what you have talked with God about throughout this chapter.

15

Living in God's Presence

 **Write.** Prayer and God's presence are two sides of the same coin. Awareness of God's presence comes as the result of taking time to speak and listen to him through prayer; conversely, the power of prayer is unleashed in the lives of those who spend time in God's presence.

When you practice being aware of God's presence, you pick up his signals all through the day. At work, at home, in your car or wherever you are, you begin to dialogue with the Lord. You share your heart with him, and you know he's listening. It has nothing to do with being in a church building or on your knees. It has to do with God's presence in and around you—"Christ in you, the hope of glory" (Colossians 1:27).

Use today as a day of "God watch." Look for God's presence in the gifts of nature around you, in the words of a friend, in an unexpected act of kindness, in a line from a book, in the trill of a songbird, in the touch of a family member, in the private inner workings of your heart. God's grace and his presence are everywhere—just watch. As you spot evidence of his presence, be ready to respond with brief words of prayer. Make notes on this page and page 120 about the events of your day.

Reflect.

When they saw the courage of Peter and John and realized that they were unschooled, ordinary men, they were astonished and they took note that these men had been with Jesus.

ACTS 4:13

❀   ❀   ❀   ❀

What kind of person are you becoming because you have "been with Jesus"?

Study.

I am the vine; you are the branches. If a man remains in me and I in him, he will bear much fruit; apart from me you can do nothing. If anyone does not remain in me, he is like a branch that is thrown away and withers; such branches are picked up, thrown into the fire and burned. If you remain in me and my words remain in you, ask whatever you wish, and it will be given you. This is to my Father's glory, that you bear much fruit, showing yourselves to be my disciples. As the Father has loved me, so have I loved you. Now remain in my love. . . . I no longer call you servants, because a servant does not know his master's business. Instead, I have called you friends, for everything that I learned from my Father I have made known to you.

J O H N 15:5-9, 15

❖ ❖ ❖ ❖

Practicing God's presence is a means of living out the intense relationship Jesus described to his disciples. Study the passage above, then write your own paraphrase—as if Jesus were speaking to you. Add explanations and personal notes as you go along. Begin by writing your name.

Prayer Journal. Meditate on each of these biblical passages about God's presence and write a prayer of response.

❊   ❊   ❊   ❊

"The virgin will be with child and will give birth to a son, and they will call him Immanuel"—which means *"God with us."*

MATTHEW 1:23

The Word became flesh and made his dwelling among us. We have seen his glory, the glory of the One and Only, who came from the Father, full of grace and truth.

JOHN 1:14

That which was from the beginning, which we have heard, which we have seen with our eyes, which we have looked at and our hands have touched—this we proclaim concerning the Word of life. The life appeared; we have seen it and testify to it, and we proclaim to you the eternal life, which was with the Father and has appeared to us.
1 J O H N 1:1-2

Record.

He who watches over you will not slumber.

PSALM 121:3

❊ ❊ ❊ ❊

Make a brief list here of what you have talked with God about throughout this chapter.